barnacle
and his friends

by Alexander Monroe

FOREWORD

This little book has been written from the point of view of the young reader. It is intended as a beginning, to help our least prejudiced citizens, the children, to appreciate the web of life here on our planet. Such a start can be made by acquainting them with some of the fascinating creatures of the shallow, intertidal waters. These organisms are grouped according to the readiness with which they may be generally found, rather than with any emphasis upon strict phylogenetic relationships.

It is hoped that "Barnacle" will lead children to consider the relationships and importance of these citizens of the sea to the overall marine ecology, rather than ask, "What good" is a mole crab, a starfish, or any other strange animal.

"Barnacle" is an imagined character illustrated by cartoon. It must be remembered that as such, he is a fantasied personality, distinct from the true barnacle.

Recognizing that such use of anthropomorphism is largely suspect among the circles of science, the author has been careful to limit the attribution of human characteristics only to "Barnacle". This technique*has been widely used as a successful method for maintaining the interest of children when introduced to a new subject area.

Barbara Waters
Marine Educator
Cape Cod Extension Service

* Sharefkin, Belle and Ruchlis, Hy. "Anthropomorphism in the Lower Grades". SCIENCE AND CHILDREN 11:37-40; March 1974. National Science Teachers Association publication.

CONTENTS

	Page 1
Devil's Purse	2
Foreword	3
This Is Barnacle	6
Barnacle's Busy World	9
Snails	15
Clams and their cousins	20
Chitons	21
Octopus & Squid	23
Crabs and their cousins	30
Horseshoe Crabs	31
Sea Urchins	32
Sand Dollars	32
Starfish	33
Sea Anemones	34
Moon Jellies	34
Comb Jellies	34
Northern Coral	34
Sponges	35
Sea Worms	36
Why are the oceans salty?	37
The Tides	38
Shell Critters	39
Scientific Names	40

this is **barnacle**

He is, in fact, a barnacle
of a most unusual kind,
for unlike his cousins who live on the beach,
he thinks with a human-like mind.

He's two inches tall and weighs half an ounce.
his head is perfectly round,
and from side to side where his ears should have been,
he wears a great big grin.

(continued next page)

His arms and legs are short and stubby.
He has no hands or feet,
just little round suction cups at the end
with which he performs some astounding feats.

He manufactures a super glue,
the strongest in the world.
He can hang on for years to the keel of a ship
and live through the very worst storm.

On top of his head, half as tall as he,
is his most remarkable feature:
a magnetic hair
with a crook in the end
that always points due North.

He's usually off on an adventure somewhere.
He's sailed all over the world.
But every Summer he returns to the North
to play with his friends on the beach.

His summer home is an old whelk shell
nestled in the cool sea grass.
Here he rests
and breathes
the fresh air.
He calls it
Barnacle's Place.

BARNACLE'S PLACE

BARNACLE'S BUSY WORLD BY THE SEA

"Barnacle's Place" is located in the great salt marsh. To the casual observer this is a very peaceful place, governed only by the wind, the sea and the sun. But, to Barnacle, it is a very busy place. Within the salt marsh, and on the nearby shore, there may be several billion little creatures industriously going about the business of making a living.

Barnacle is frequently awakened by battalions of fiddler crabs as they march by Barnacle's Place on the way to the creek. He can hear a hermit crab as it clumps along carrying its house on its back. He can also see thousands of periwinkles scraping nearby rocks and hear millions of barnacles clicking their trap doors shut as the tide recedes.

Barnacle likes to race with sandpipers on the open beach as they dart in and out with the waves. He plays tag with razor clams on the tidal flats as they poke up out of the sand, and has digging contests with mole crabs at the waters edge. On the upper beach, he tries to outjump the sandhoppers which can leap 50 times their own length.

The creek is always making bubbling sounds as

the tide flows in and out. Barnacle likes to hop onto the edge of a little whirlpool, as he floats up the creek to a little harbor, and spin around until he is dizzy.

In the harbor, Barnacle enjoys looking at the sea anemones which have beautiful flower-like fans and are often attached to the pilings and docks. Barnacle thinks the teredos (shipworms) are great sculptors. He helps them chisel out fascinating designs in pilings and in the hulls of wooden boats.

His marine world also includes any rivers, sand dunes or grassy areas that are influenced by the saltwater or seawind. Barnacle would have to sail over 88,600 miles just to cover the shoreline of the United States. He would have to sail nearly a million miles to cover the shoreline of the whole world, which would stretch from here to the moon over three and a half times.

If you multiplied the billions of animals that live in any one mile of Barnacle's world by the total number of miles in his world the number would be so large it would be hard to understand. But two things are certain: even if Barnacle doesn't know what it all adds up to, there are a lot of hearts beating in Barnacle's world by the sea and it is, indeed, a very busy place.

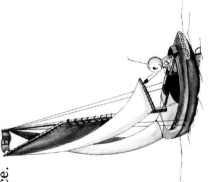

There is also the very serious game of hide and seek Barnacle plays with the sea gulls and terns which are always on the scene looking for a tender morsel to swallow.

There is a certain rhythm of smells and sounds along the shore which Barnacle finds exciting. This rhythm speeds up during the late spring and summer months, but in the fall this rhythm slows down. Some of his friends hibernate in the marsh mud during the winter. Others fly south, swim out to deeper water (where it is warmer) or slow down their activities during the cold months.

Barnacle often sails his little sloop to other parts of his world by the sea, which extends all along the shores of all the islands and continents on earth.

MOLLUSKS

Mollusks are soft-bodied animals that have no backbone. Most of them grow shells and have a large, fleshy foot with which they move. They are divided into different groups according to the way they build their shells, although one mollusk, the octopus, no longer grows a shell. Snails, clams, oysters, chitons and squids are all mollusks.

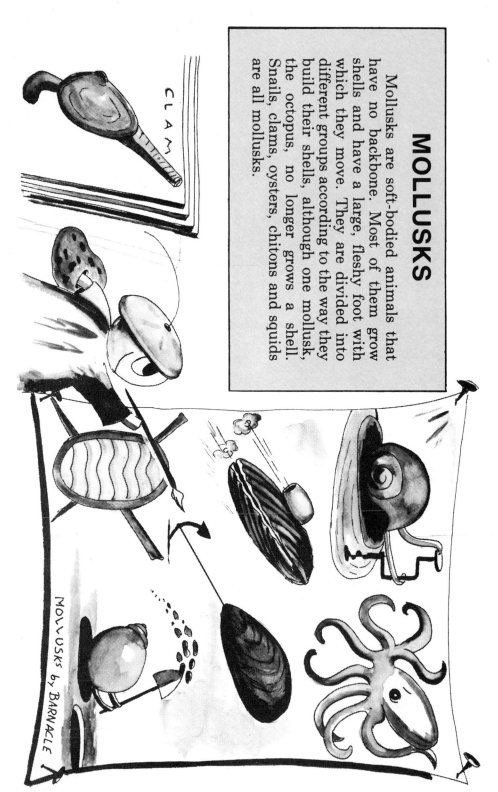

CLAM

MOLLUSKS by BARNACLE

periwinkles
and other little snails

periwinkles
less than 1 inch (2.5 cm)

Although there are 12 species of periwinkles that live along the Atlantic coast, the one you are most likely to find is the common periwinkle. They are rather dull in color and are often found in the barnacle zone scraping algae off rocks with their long, rasping (sandpaper) tongues. Periwinkles are a favorite seafood in Europe, and good to eat here, too.

oyster drill
less than 1 inch (2.5 cm)

This is a pretty, little snail with a sculptured shell. It can be found looking for oysters or other shellfish. Oyster drills get their food by drilling holes through other animals' shells.

SNAILS

There are over 80,000 different kinds of snails. They are called univalves, which means "one shell." Some are as small as a grain of sand. Others are more than 2 feet long. While many snails live on land and breathe air, most live in either fresh or salt water. Most of the large snails live in salt water.

Barnacle is always careful about what kind of snail with which he associates because one thing all snails have in common is a long, file-like tongue. Some snails use their tongues only to scrape up plant food from rocks. Others, however, are meat-eating (carnivorous) and spend most of their time drilling holes in other animals' shells.

Most snails have a coiled, or twisted shell. Those without a coil in their shells are called limpets. Many snails make interesting egg cases to protect their young until they hatch.

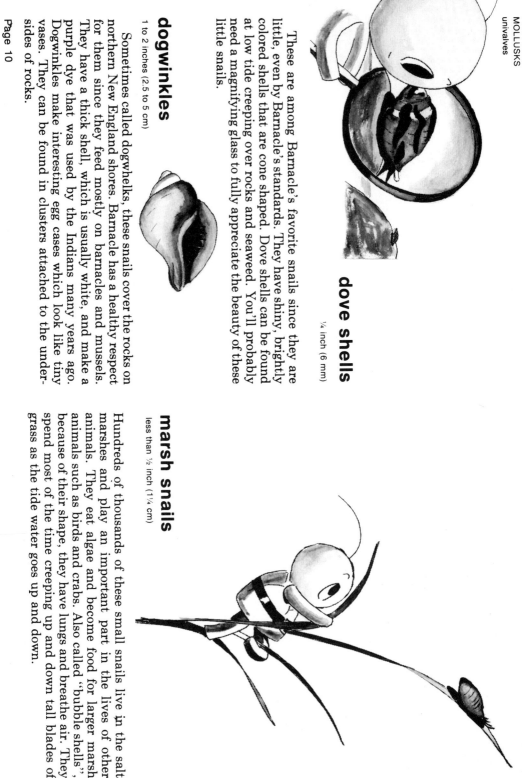

dove shells

¼ inch (6 mm)

These are among Barnacle's favorite snails since they are little, even by Barnacle's standards. They have shiny, brightly colored shells that are cone shaped. Dove shells can be found at low tide creeping over rocks and seaweed. You'll probably need a magnifying glass to fully appreciate the beauty of these little snails.

dogwinkles

1 to 2 inches (2.5 to 5 cm)

Sometimes called dogwhelks, these snails cover the rocks on northern New England shores. Barnacle has a healthy respect for them since they feed mostly on barnacles and mussels. They have a thick shell, which is usually white, and make a purple dye that was used by the Indians many years ago. Dogwinkles make interesting egg cases which look like tiny vases. They can be found in clusters attached to the undersides of rocks.

marsh snails

less than ½ inch (1¼ cm)

Hundreds of thousands of these small snails live in the salt marshes and play an important part in the lives of other animals. They eat algae and become food for larger marsh animals such as birds and crabs. Also called "bubble shells", because of their shape, they have lungs and breathe air. They spend most of the time creeping up and down tall blades of grass as the tide water goes up and down.

mud snails
up to 1 inch (2.5 cm)

Mud snails can be found by the thousands at low tide on mud flats where fresh water flows into the sea. They are about the same color as the mud they live on, usually brown. They help keep mud flats clean by scavenging for decaying animal and plant life. They will also attack live animals, but this is rare. Their shells are usually eroded in places which makes them look rather worn out.

waved whelks
up to 3 inches (7.5 cm)

The rather thick shells of this animal have a more pronounced coil than most northern shells. They are carnivorous and live in deeper tidal pools, or offshore. Their yellowish egg capsules are about the size of a split pea and can often be found washed up on the beach. They will be attached together in masses the size of a baseball. These masses of egg cases used to be called "sailors' soap" since they will foam up when rubbed. Old time sailors used them to clean dirty hands.

It's easy for Barnacle to organize an army of small snails for a parade along the beach

whelks

knobbed and channeled

up to 9 inches (22.5 cm)

Except for the horseshoe crab, these are the largest of Barnacle's friends in the northeast (from Cape Cod south). They eat clams and other shellfish by either prying open their victims' shells with their own big shell or by drilling holes with their sharp tongues.

Knobbed whelks are slightly larger than channeled whelks and the inner shell is often colored a bright, reddish orange. Channeled whelks are usually yellowish inside.

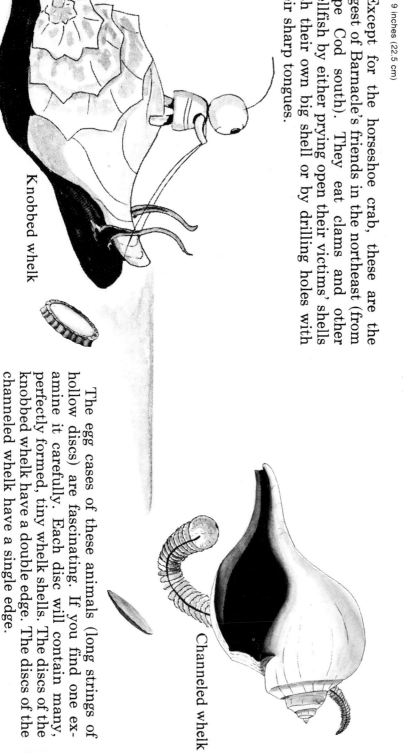

Knobbed whelk

Channeled whelk

The egg cases of these animals (long strings of hollow discs) are fascinating. If you find one examine it carefully. Each disc will contain many, perfectly formed, tiny whelk shells. The discs of the knobbed whelk have a double edge. The discs of the channeled whelk have a single edge.

moon snails
and sand collars
up to 4 inches (10 cm)

The moon snail has a large, round shell. Barnacle won't be caught napping around these snails since they are efficient drillers and get their food by drilling holes in other animals shells. You don't have to worry, though. They won't hurt you.

Barnacle thinks moon snails are good architects. To protect their eggs they glue together a big collar of sand and deposit their eggs within the wall of this collar. Look for these collars on sandy, flat areas of the beach at low tide.

If you want to preserve a sand collar let it dry until it is just barely damp. Then paint it with white glue and let it dry. After the glue is dry paint or spray the collar with a clear varnish.

boat shells

quarterdecks

up to 2 inches (5 cm)

The boat shell is one of the most plentiful shells on the beach. It is a snail without a coil, called a limpet. The shell is usually speckled brown, and on the inside there is a hard, white platform that looks like the quarterdeck of a ship. If the shell is well balanced it makes a perfect little ship with accommodations for about one small periwinkle.

The snail that makes this shell leads a very quiet life, even for a snail. It attaches itself to an object, such as a rock or another boat shell, and lives there for the rest of its life. The edge of the shell grows to fit the object to which it is attached. Boat shells usually pile up in heaps, one shell on top of another.

slipper shells

The slipper shell is related to the boat shell but is much flatter. It spends its life inside other shells, cans or anything else into which it can creep.

Chinaman's hat

limpet

up to 1 inch (2.5 cm)

Like the boat shell, the chinaman's hat limpet doesn't have a coil in its shell, but it is a univalve just like periwinkles and whelks. It has a powerful foot with which it clings to rocks, shells or other hard objects, and creeps about slowly as it scrapes seaweed with its long, sandpaper tongue. You need a great deal of patience to see a limpet move.

Although limpets in the northeast are small there are different kinds of limpets in other parts of the world that are as large as your fist.

clams

soft shelled clams

1 to 6 inches (2.5 to 15 cm)

These are the most popular for eating and can be found under the surface of the sand or mud when the tide is out. As you walk along look for little squirts of water which come from the clams' siphons.

surf clams

up to 7 inches (17.5 cm)

Also called sea clams, these bivalves are most comonly found very low in the intertidal zone or in deeper water. You can often locate them by standing in shallow water at low tide and poking your toes down into the sand. They make the largest shell you will find on North Atlantic beaches. They are very good to eat in pies and chowders but are not as popular as soft shelled clams or quahogs.

BIVALVES

Bivalves are animals with two shells. Though some live in fresh water, most bivalves live in Barnacle's world at the edge of the sea. There are also many deep water varieties that live offshore. Bivalves vary in size from a fraction of an inch to more than 4 feet long (in the wstern Pacific ocean), and include clams, oysters, mussels and scallops. Most bivalves use their large, fleshy foot for digging or pulling themselves down into the sand. Different kinds of bivalves can swim by jet propulsion, burrow, anchor themselves with thread or live on the underwater parts of trees or wooden structures. Like snails, many bivalves make beautifully marked shells which have been copied by artists ever since man first started drawing pictures.

Barnacle feels completely safe around bivalves since they are not hunters like many of the snails. They get their food simply by sucking in water through a siphon tube and filtering out thousands of microscopic animals and plants.

The hinge that connects the bivalve's two shells is elastic and will hold the shells open. To close their shells bivalves use one or two powerful muscles which are attached to the inside of both shells.

quahogs *(pronounced co-hogs)*

3 to 5 inches (7.5 to 12.5 cm)

These are hard shelled clams. Smaller sizes are called littlenecks or cherrystones, delicious when eaten raw. Larger quahogs make good chowders. Quahogs can be found just under the surface of the sand or mud in saltwater bays and ponds. Indians made "wampum" from the purple parts of the larger quahog shells.

oysters

2 to 6 inches (5 to 15 cm)

Oysters grow attached to rocks and other solid objects. You will find their shells washed up on the beach. Each shell has its own interesting form shaped by the object upon which it grows. To Barnacle they look more like rocks than shellfish.

mussels

1 to 3 inches (2.5 to 7.5 cm)

There are whole cities of blue mussels crowded together on rocky areas or on the pilings of docks. They anchor themselves with strong threads (byssus) which hold them from being washed away by the tide. The inside of the shell is the color of a shiny pearl. There are also ribbed mussels which anchor themselves in saltmarsh peat and larger horse mussels which are most common in colder waters. Occasionally a horse mussel shell will wash up on the beach.

bay scallops

up to 3 inches (7.5 cm)

The shell of this animal is shaped like a fan and each has its own individual coloring. No two are alike. Bay scallops prefer shallow water and swim by jet propulsion, forcing water out as they open and close their shells. If you observe them under-water they look like sets of false teeth clacking away. You will notice rows of blue eyes at the edge of the shell. The round, white muscle that holds the shells together is the delicious 'scallop' which many people like to eat.

SHELLFISH LICENSES

Check with your local shellfish warden before digging live shellfish. A license is required in most cases.

False angel wings
to 2 inches (5 cm)

Watch out for Barnacle when he's wearing angel wings because he's probably up to no good. The wings that Barnacle is wearing are called false angel wings and are made by a clam that burrows deep in the mud, peat or clay. They resemble the shells of a larger, more spectacular animal of a different family called angel wings, rarely found north of Virginia.

Like the true angel wing, the shell of this animal is chalky white and quite interesting with its wing-like shape and ridges. It can be found on the beach or in the salt marshes at low tide. You'll have quite a prize if you can find a pair still hinged together.

razor clams
up to 10 inches (25 cm)

These clams look like the old fashioned, straight razor and live standing up in the sand. When they feed, two siphons pull in water (containing food) through a hole in the sand. They can dig very fast with a wedge shaped, shovel foot and may disappear in a hurry.

gem shells
less than ¼ inch (6 mm)

These shells are so small you are liable to regard them as just part of the sand unless you have been told they are there. Amethyst as a color is purple and so are many of these little shells. In Long Island Sound they are mostly white. Often confused with young quahogs, gem shells can be found on some beaches in great quantities, often so numerous that the larvae*(young stages) of other clams can not find a place on which to settle.

Early settlers in New England sent boxes of these shells back to England as curiosities.

* See "Larvae", Inside back cover.

jingle shells

under 2 inches (5 cm)

JINGLE
JINGLE
JINGLE

These are thin little shells with a waxy luster which, according to Barnacle, make the "best darn jingle this side of the Sargasso Sea." They are plentiful and come in a variety of colors: yellow, silver, copper, gray and black.

Jingle shells are true bivalves, although you'll rarely find both shells. The animal lives in shallow water attached, through a hole, to a rock or some other object. The bottom shell is flat and usually so firmly attached that only the top shell will wash ashore.

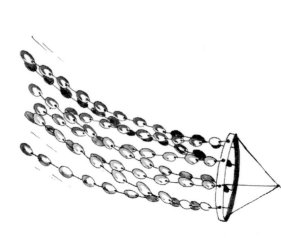

teredos
(*shipworms*)

Shell: ¼ inch (6 mm);
Animal: up to 3 inches (7.5 cm)

According to Barnacle these animals are great artists. Though they may look like worms to some people, they are really long clams with two small shells near the head which they use like a sculptor's chisel. They cut beautiful designs in anything wooden.

Barnacle lived with teredos back in the old days of wooden sailing ships. When Barnacle was serving on the bottom of the *Golden Hind*, the first English ship to sail around the world in 1580, there were teredos inside chiseling out beautiful designs in the planking. Trouble came later on when the designs took up more space than the planking, and the *Golden Hind* collapsed.

You will frequently see the work of these animals in driftwood washed up on the beach.

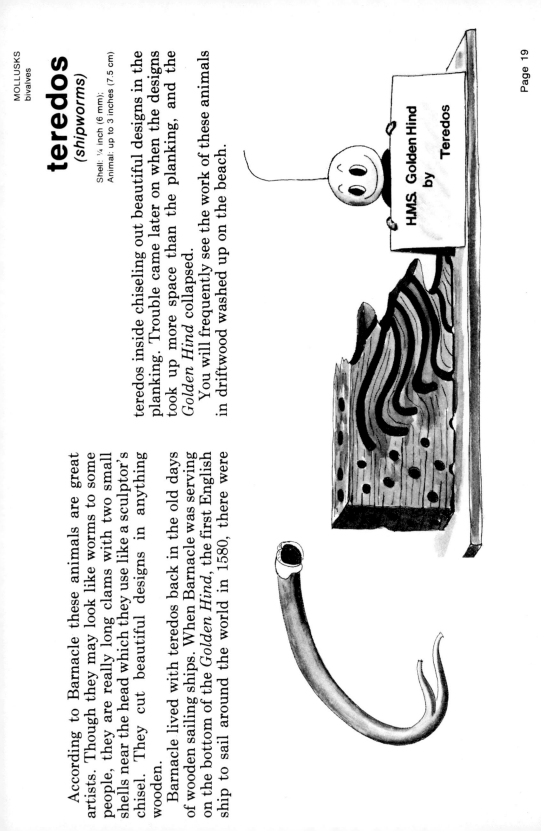

H.M.S. Golden Hind
by Teredos

chitons *(pronounced ki-tons)*

up to 1 inch (2.5 cm)

Barnacle had never paid much attention to his friends, the chitons, until he read that they have lived one life style and remained unchanged for the past 500,000,000 years. Quite different from man who has changed from a sea animal, to a crawling land animal, to a tree animal, to an ape-like animal

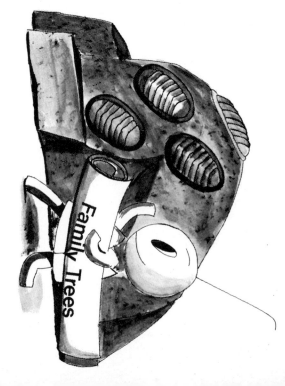

Family Trees

before becoming man. Even barnacles and horseshoe crabs can't claim a life style as old as the chiton.

Chitons are mollusks in a class all by themselves and can be found on shells thrown up on the beach, or on rocks in shallow water at low tide. They have a shell made up of 8 overlapping plates which allow the animal to bend like a coat of mail (chain-like armor worn by knights many years ago). Chitons lead a rather quiet life sticking pretty much to one rcck or shell. If you pick one up it will roll into a ball.

squid *and* octopus

Squid: 8 to 20 inches (20 to 50 cm)
Octopus: usually no larger than a basketball

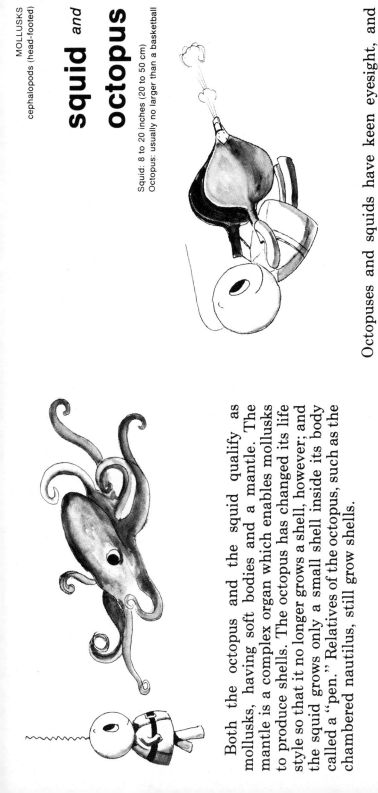

Both the octopus and the squid qualify as mollusks, having soft bodies and a mantle. The mantle is a complex organ which enables mollusks to produce shells. The octopus has changed its life style so that it no longer grows a shell, however; and the squid grows only a small shell inside its body called a "pen." Relatives of the octopus, such as the chambered nautilus, still grow shells.

Octopuses and squids have keen eyesight, and can swim by jet propulsion, backwards. They can change color when excited or feeding. When the squid is threatened by an enemy it squirts out a smoke-screen of inky fluid and hides behind it.

Although there are squids in deep water which reach a length of over 50 feet, most stories about giant squids and octopuses are exaggerated.

ARTHROPODS

Arthropods include about three quarters of the animals living on earth, about 600,000 species. They all have hard, outside skeletons that are divided into a number of jointed parts. They live everywhere, on land and in fresh and salt water. Arthropods include insects, spiders, centipedes and crustaceans.

An arthropod can not expand beyond the limits of its hard shell. In order to grow it must crawl out of its hard shell (molt) and grow in a hurry before its new shell becomes hard. Some animals expand as much as one third their body size immediately after crawling out of their shells.

CRUSTACEANS

Crustaceans are arthropods that have gills, antennae and jointed legs. They include the crabs, lobsters, shrimps, barnacles and sandhoppers.

swimming crabs

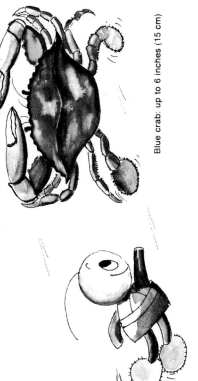

Blue crab: up to 6 inches (15 cm)

Swimming crabs have rear legs that are flattened into paddles. They can dart very quickly through the water, swimming sideways.. The largest and best known swimming crab is the blue crab. It is the most popular for eating, especially just after molting when it is caught and sold as a soft-shelled crab. Blue crabs can be found in many areas; however, pollution of our rivers and bays has greatly reduced their numbers.

The calico crab (lady crab) is a smaller swimming crab. It has a rounder shell with a speckled pattern on the back.

CRABS

When a man referred to one of Barnacle's crab friends as an "ugly little crab", it made Barnacle very sad. It's true that crabs aren't the friendliest looking creatures in the world, and Barnacle has a lot of respect for their "pinch", but he doesn't think the word "ugly" is appropriate. "Remarkable" would be a better term. For instance, when any of his crab friends lose a claw Barnacle never sees them moping about feeling sorry for themselves. The old claw will be replaced by a new one. This is called "regeneration," one of the biggest mysteries in biology.

Calico crab: up to 3 inches (7.5 cm)

hermit crabs

about 2¼ inches (5.5 cm)

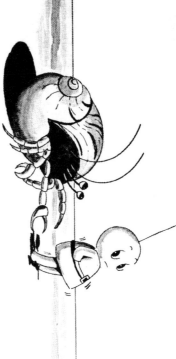

These entertaining, little creatures are every-where, in small tidal pools or shallow water close to shore. They climb into unoccupied snail shells, and hook themselves in tightly with the soft part of their bodies. When they walk their house goes along with them.

A small hermit may start living in a periwinkle shell, but as it grows it must move into larger quarters such as a moon snail shell or whelk shell.

* See "Snail Fur", Inside back cover.

fiddler crabs

about 1 inch (2.5 cm)

These little crabs live in burrows up to 3 feet deep. You can often see their holes dotting the marshes at low tide. The male fiddler has a very large claw which it often waves back and forth in the fashion of a violin player. Actually it is only used to wave to female fiddlers and for a little fighting during mating season. Fiddler crabs are quite gregarious and often march over the sand, or through the marsh grass, in great armies. When they dig their burrows they roll the mud or sand up into little balls and deposit them neatly just outside their holes.

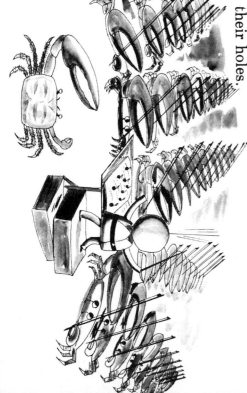

rock crabs

up to 5 inches (12.5 cm)

These are red spotted crabs which can be found in shallow water under rocks. They can be eaten but are not as popular as the blue crab.

spider crabs

about 5 inches (12.5 cm)

Spider crabs can be found in shallow, salt water ponds. They look a lot like spiders, having a small, round shell and long spindly legs. Their claws are rather small and weak. Discarded shells are often washed up on the beach.

Though these crabs seldom reach large sizes in North Atlantic waters, Barnacle has seen spider crabs 12 feet in diameter in the western Pacific ocean.

mole crabs

up to 1 inch (2.5 cm)

Sometimes known as sand bugs, these little crabs can be found in great numbers on beaches from the south shore of Cape Cod and to the south. You will rarely see them unless you dig. They live at the water's edge and travel back and forth, under the sand, as the tide moves in and out. Two shovel-like feet enable this little animal to dig very rapidly, backwards.

lobsters

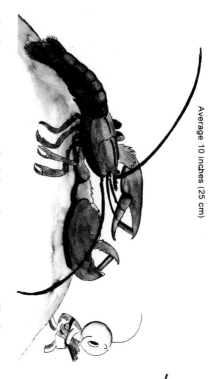

Average 10 inches (25 cm)

Lobsters are probably the most well known crustacean since they are so delicious to eat. There are stories that the Indians and Pilgrims used to pick lobsters from under inshore rocks at low tide, but so many of them have been caught, it isn't likely you'll see one today unless it's in a fish market or on the dinner table. Small lobsters, up to a few pounds, are caught in wooden traps by lobster fishermen not far from shore. Giants are caught well out to sea. Live lobsters are green. They turn bright red when cooked.

sand shrimp

about 1¾ inches (3 cm)

If you feel something tickling your toes when you're standing at the water's edge it will probably be a common sand shrimp. They populate sandy areas and tidal pools. Though they move very quickly they are easy to catch and make good fish bait. Striped bass, bluefish and flounder are known to hunt these little animals.

sand hoppers

less than 1 inch (2.5 cm)

Sand hoppers are among Barnacle's most lively playmates. They can jump 50 times their own length. Also known as beach fleas, they live near the ocean but can't stay in the water very long. They look for food at night when they are safe from swooping birds and when the tide is out. During the day they retreat above high tide, and burrow in the sand, headfirst. On a warm evening the beach seems to come alive with these hopping creatures.

Sand hoppers are in the evolutionary process of crawling out of the sea and becoming land animals. They still have gills for breathing and obtain oxygen from moist air in the damp sand. Look for their big, blue eyes.

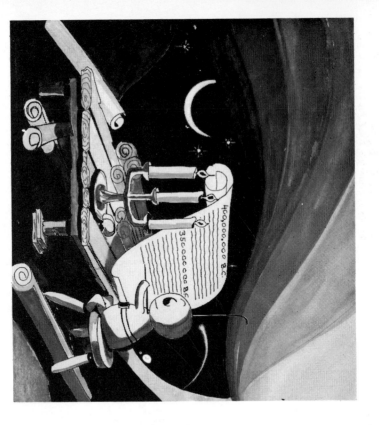

his cousins, the
barnacles

usually less than ½ inch (1¼ cm)
(can be larger)

Barnacle is very proud of his ancient ancestry which goes back 400 million years, long before the dinosaurs, (man is only a few million years old). Frequently Barnacle will sit up all night working on his family tree just to prove that a barnacle's life style is older than that of his friend, the horseshoe crab, which is so well known for its ancient ancestry.

Although there are many different kinds of barnacles living in the sea the kind we see the most is the acorn barnacle which lives in the "splash zone," somewhere between high tide and low. There are trillions upon trillions of barnacles living all over the world. Some scientists call this "The Age of Barnacles."

All barnacles make a super glue with which they cement themselves to just about anything in the

goose barnacles

up to 2 inches (5 cm)

ocean, from cola cans to whales, and including glass, wood, metal, concrete and plastic.

If man could make glue as strong as a barnacle's (which sticks to anything) he could glue together broken bones and make everyone's teeth as good as new.

Although barnacles can swim about freely when they are very young (without their shells) once they settle down and start building their limestone houses they become fixed to one spot for the rest of their lives.

Actually barnacles live upside down, standing on their heads. They open their trap doors only when the tide is in, and kick food into their mouths with their feathery feet. Barnacles have jointed bodies, like other crustaceans, and molt as they grow, even inside their houses.

In the summer when the water is warm, goose barnacles can often be found attached by long, slender stalks to the under side of floating objects. Because of the gooseneck stalk and the feathery feet, which look like the tail feathers of a young bird, some people in Europe (during the 1500's) used to think a certain sea bird, the barnacle goose, actually hatched from goose barnacles.

The barnacle goose was considered a fish for a time and the Catholic Church allowed the eating of this bird during the Lenten season when it was customary to eat only fish. Even as late as the early 1900's people in certain parts of Ireland continued the custom although the fairytale had long since been exposed.

But, as Barnacle always says: "once a barnacle, always a barnacle and never a goose."

really not crabs

horseshoe crabs

up to 20 inches (50 cm)

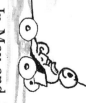

Horseshoe crabs are not crabs. Nor are they crustaceans. They belong to a class of animals called the arachnids, most of which live on land, including the scorpions and spiders.

Horseshoe crabs are very ancient creatures, having remained unchanged for hundreds of millions of years. Although they are strange looking they are harmless. Their tails enable them to steer and to right themselves.

These animals can be found along sand or mud flats and in calm water near the saltmarshes. It is interesting to find the cast off shell left after molting. Every detail of the animal's body is evident in the cast off shell. Unlike crabs which back out of their shells, horseshoe crabs crawl out the front.

In May and June horseshoe crabs may be found in pairs as they mate. The larger female, carrying the male with her, crawls up to the high tide mark, digs a hole and lays eggs the size of apple seeds. The male then fertilizes them. In a month or less the eggs will hatch into tiny, fingernail-size horseshoe crabs without tails, and will be carried to sea by the next spring tide.

sea urchins

1½ to 3 inches (3¾ to 7.5 cm)

Sea urchins are made up of five curved plates which are joined together to form a slightly flattened, ball-like skeleton. They can be found in dark corners clinging to rocks or pilings just below the low tide mark. The movable spines feel sharp, but urchins in the northeast are not dangerous.

These animals have tube feet with suction cups which enable them to hang on tightly so they won't be washed away by the waves. Green sea urchins are found in the colder waters north of Cape Cod. Most sea urchins found south of Cape Cod are purple. When they die the spines drop off leaving a skeleton which looks like a speckled ball.

ECHINODERMS

Echinoderms are exclusively salt water animals. They are known for their radial symmetry, that is having a number of equal parts, spreading out from the center like the spokes of a wheel, or slices of a pie. Echinoderms have five parts and a central mouth. The name echino (spiny) and derm (skin) describes them well since their body surface is covered with spines.

star fish

6 to 11 inches (15 to 27.5 cm)

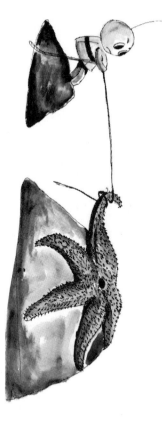

The common starfish most often found has five arms, although there are starfish with ten or more arms. Starfish have spines on their backs and suction cups on their feet like sea urchins and sand dollars. A starfish can wrap itself around a clam and pull it open. It then eats the clam.

If a starfish loses an arm it will grow a new one, although the new arm may not grow as big as the original arm. The orange spot on the back of the animal is not an eye, but a sieve plate through which water enters the body. The red and orange, dot-sized eyes are located at the ends of the five arms.

sand dollars

up to 3 inches (7.5 cm)

Sand dollars are related to sea urchins, though they are much flatter and their spines much shorter. They look like big coins and have the design of a five petaled flower on their backs. Although they live in deeper water, half buried in the sand, you can often find them washed up on sandy, flat areas at very low tide. If dried in the sun they will turn white. They are fun to collect, although they are quite fragile.

Although they are too dull and slow for him to play with, Barnacle has collected a fortune in sand dollars.

sea anemones

up to 4 inches (10 cm)

CNIDARIA

Cnidaria (pronounced ni-daria) are primitive animals that have tentacles and stinging cells for capturing food, and one, large cavity inside the body. Like echinoderms, they also are known for their radial symmetry. Many cnidaria are considered quite beautiful because of their brilliant coloring.

When open, these creatures, with their waving tentacles, look like flowers. When feeding, disturbed or left high and dry by the tide, they usually close by pulling in their tentacles. Anemones can be found at the low tide mark attached to rocks and pilings. They can also be found on the undersides of floating docks.

Sea anemones commonly reproduce sexually, making new individuals from fertilized eggs. They may also grow new animals at the base. There are sea anemones that can split in half to make two, and Barnacle has often wondered if these anemones ever grow old.

northern coral

Individual animal 1 / 8 inch (3 mm)

Most people associate coral with warm water and reefs, but there are corals that grow in colder, northern waters. One coral you are likely to see, star coral, grows in colonies, or groups, no larger than the size of your hand. It can be found just below the lowest tide mark attached to rocks. Coral colonies are made up of small individual animals each of which builds its own little limestone house. Each coral animal has its own set of stinging cells with which it captures small swimming organisms in the water for food.

moon jellies

3 to 9 inches (7.5 to 22.5 cm)

This is a jellyfish which you'll frequently see in shallow salt ponds in late spring. It is interesting to observe from above, from a boat or dock. Moon jellies vary in color (white, pink and orange) and will frequently wash up on the beach where they look like globs of jelly. Sets of horseshoe shaped gonads (used for reproduction) can be seen through their transparent bodies, which are more than 95% water. They will not sting you.

comb jellies

about 6 inches (15 cm)

This animal looks like jelly but it is not related to the moon jelly. It comes from an entirely different group of animals (ctenophora) since it doesn't have stinging cells and has only one set of tentacles. Comb jellies are a beautiful sight to behold, especially on a moon lit night when they shine as pulsating globs of light. They have 8 rows of beating cilia (hairs) to help them move.

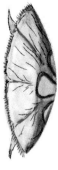

deadman's finger

Deadman's fingers are often washed up on the beach after a storm. They look like large brown fingers full of tiny holes and live offshore in the colder waters of the North Atlantic coast.

PORIFERA

The term porifera means "full of holes." These are the sponges which look more like plants than animals. They attach themselves to rocks, or to the sea bottom. Sponges are colonies of single cells growing together. Each group of cells does a different task such as getting food or reproducing.

You won't see the popular "bath sponge" in northern waters. However, some sponges may be found washed up on the beach.

boring sponge

This sponge settles on mollusk shells and, as it grows, bores the shells full of holes. You will often see the riddled shells on the beach.

redbeard sponge

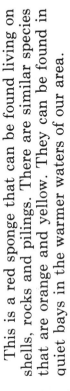

This is a red sponge that can be found living on shells, rocks and pilings. There are similar species that are orange and yellow. They can be found in quiet bays in the warmer waters of our area.

ANNELIDS

These are the segmented worms which live both on land and in water. Annelids that live in the sea (sea worms) are likely to be much more unusual and colorful than their dull cousins, the earthworms.

decorator* worm

up to 12 inches (30 cm)

In tidal pools, and just below the low tide mark in shallow water, you can often see little bits of shells and other debris glued together in a tube-like mass, 2 or 3 inches high. This is the "chimney" of the decorator worm's house, a tube that may extend 3 feet down into the sand. This animal is quite beautiful when it extends its scarlet head out of the tube to feed or collect more debris.

clam worm

up to 18 inches (45 cm)

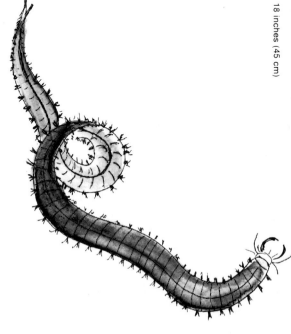

These are the bait worms (sold as sea worms) that are so popular with salt water fishermen. Soft bristles extend from each segment all along the sides of their bodies. Clam worms are noted for a hidden pair of sharp pincers which can extend rapidly from their mouths and give you quite a nip. They live in the sand by day and swim about at night looking for food.

lug worm

6 to 8 inches (15 to 20 cm)

Lug worms live in the sand and feed on minute organic material below. You can often see little tubes of sand coiled up in a heap on sandy tidal flats. These are made by the lug worm as it burrows in the sand below.

limy tube worms

up to 3 inches (7.5 cm)

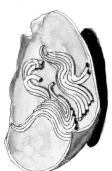

You will often see twisted masses of small calcium tubes coiled on mollusk shells. These are the homes of the limy tube worms. They spread colorful fans of feathery tentacles from the tubes, and disappear in a hurry when startled.

WHY ARE THE OCEANS SALTY?

For as long as there have been land and sea the rivers of the world have been washing salt (and other minerals, too) into the oceans. At first (many hundreds of millions of years ago) the oceans weren't very salty since not very much salt had been washed into the sea. Now, ocean water is so salty we can't drink it.

Just as the rivers are pouring millions of gallons of water (containing salt and minerals) into the oceans every day, millions of gallons of water from the oceans are evaporating into the air every day and being redistributed over the land in the form of rain. Since salt can't evaporate it stays in the ocean.

Today's rain will make tomorrow's rivers and carry even more salt into the oceans. Since the process of rain and evaporation is going on all the time the oceans are salty and becoming saltier and saltier every day.

The next time you spend some time on the beach fill a small shell with ocean water and put it aside in the sun to dry. The water will evaporate and leave a small deposit of salt in the shell.

The Tides

The gravity of both the moon and the sun is constantly pulling at earth, causing the ocean water to go up and down (in and out) all along the shores of the world. This rising and falling of ocean water is called "tides"; *high tide* when the water is at its highest, and *low tide* when the water is at its lowest. In the northeastern United States there are two high tides and two low tides about every 25 hours, which makes each tide approximately an hour later every day.

Twice every month, at the new moon and full moon, the moon lines up with the sun allowing both bodies to pull together. When this happens, "spring tides" occur, where the high tides are higher than normal, and the low tides, lower. Other conditions such as the wind and shape of the ocean bottom can also affect tides.

The intertidal zone (which Barnacle likes to think of as the "barnacle zone") is that area of shore between high and low tide. This area and the shallow waters just offshore are the home of all the animals described in this book.

Many of the animals spawn (lay eggs), change color or develop other habits according to a strict time table based on the tides, setting their "biological clocks" to the tidal rhythms of their home beaches. Some animals continue to live by the same time table even if transported well inland. There are animals whose "clocks" are so accurate you could set your watch by them.

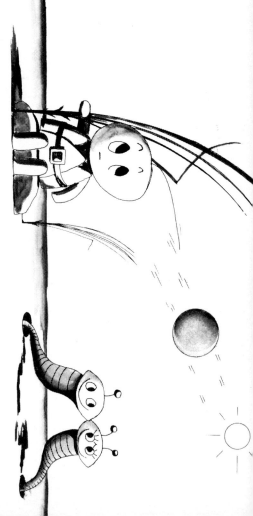

SHELL CRITTERS

It's fun to make critters from seashells. All you need are some shells, a little glue and some imagina-tion. Here are two beasts that Barnacle made to scare spooks away from from Barnacle's Place.

the whelk man

HAT - clam shell
WINGS and FEET
    - mussel shells
BODY - whelk shells
LEGS - straw from
      beach grass
EYES and SOCKS
      - paint

You can make the Whelk Man without straw legs. Just glue the mussel shells directly to the lower part of the bottom whelk shell.

googly eyes

Googly eyes is easy to make. You'll need two scallop shells, two mussel shells and two periwinkle shells. Each pair of shells should be about the same size. You'll also need some dried seaweed, paint and glue.

The only trouble Barnacle had when he made Googly Eyes was making him look mean.

SCIENTIFIC NAMES

Page 1   Skate egg case case *Raja*
Page 9   Periwinkle *Littorina*
          Oyster Drill *Urosalpinx*
Page 10   Marsh Snail *Melampus*
          Dogwinkle *Nucella*
          Dove Shell *Anachis*
Page 11   Mud Snail *Nassarius*
          Waved Whelk *Buccinum*
Page 12   Knobbed Whelk *Busycon carica*
          Channeled Whelk
          Busycon canaliculatum
Page 13   Moon Snail *Lunatia or Polinices*
Page 14   Boat Shell *Crepidula*
          Limpet *Acmaea*
Page 15   Soft Shelled Clam *Mya*
          Surf Clam *Spisula*
Page 16   Quahog *Mercenaria*
          Oyster *Crassostrea*
          Scallop *Aequipecten*
          Blue Mussel *Mytilus*
          Ribbed Mussel *Modiolus*
Page 17   False Angel Wing *Petricola*
          Gem Shell *Gemma*
          Razor Clam *Ensis*
Page 18   Jingle Shell *Anomia*
Page 19   Teredo *Teredo*
Page 20   Chiton *Chaetopleura*
Page 21   Octopus *Octopus*
          Squid *Loligo*

Page 23   Blue Crab *Callinectes*
          Calico Crab *Ovalipes*
Page 24   Hermit Crab *Pagarus*
          Fiddler Crab *Uca*
Page 25   Spider Crab *Libinia*
          Rock Crab *Cancer*
          Mole Crab *Emerita*
Page 26   Lobster *Homarus*
          Sand Shrimp *Palaemonetes*
          Sand Hopper*Talorchestia*
Page 27   Acorn Barnacle *Balanus*
Page 28   Goose Barnacle *Lepas*
Page 29   Horseshoe Crab *Limulus*
Page 30   Sea Urchin *Arabacia* &
Page 31   *Strongylocentrotus*
          Star Fish *Asterias*
Page 32   Sand Dollar *Echinarachnus*
Page 33   Sea Anemone *Metridium*
          Northern Coral *Astrangia*
Page 34   Moon Jelly *Aurelia*
          Comb Jelly *Pleurobrachia*
Page 35   Deadman's Fingers *Haliclona*
          Redbeard Sponge *Microciona*
          Boring Sponge *Cliona*
Page 36   Limy Tube Worm *Hydroides*
          Clam Worm *Nereis*
Page 37   Lug Worm *Arenicola*
          Decorator Worm *Diopatra*